Talk to Me 2

2ND Edition

Happy House

Contents

Talk to Me 2

Story Making

Debate

Syllabus

Unit	Title	Talking About	Example
01	It Is a Happy Sunny Day	pictures	• There are four trees in front of the house. In the garden, a man is watering the plants. It is a sunny day. It is a happy picture.
02	Do Not Touch!	signs and rules	• Do not take photos. • You should be quiet.
03	Where Is the Cafeteria?	directions	• The cafeteria is on the third floor. Go up the stairs. Turn left and go straight. It is on your left. You can't miss it.
04	What Is This For?	objects	• I draw or write with pencils. They are made of wood and lead. We can see pencils at home, school, and work.
05	They Are Similar but Different	similarities and differences	• The lemon is yellow. The banana is yellow too. But one is sour and the other is sweet.
06	Imagine This!	possible or impossible situations	• I would like superpowers. • I would wish for a lot of computer games.
07	I Would Rather Choose This	preferences	• I would rather have only daytime. • I would rather have only nighttime.
08	She Needs Some Advice	advice	• Why don't you hide the bag? • You should tell her not to take your things.

Unit	Title	Talking About	Example
09	What Do You Know about It?	facts and opinions	• Rabbits have a short tail and long ears. • I think rabbits are the best animals because they are cute.
10	This Happened Yesterday	the past (what, when)	• I fell off my bike yesterday. I hurt my knee. • Last weekend, I fell off my bike. I broke my wrist.
11	We Met at the School Yard	the past (who, where, why)	• On my first day of school, my mom walked with me to school. I was nervous because everything was new to me.
12	Tell Me How to Make Milk Tea	instructions	• First, boil the water. Second, put the tea bag in a cup. Third, pour the hot water and wait. Last, remove the tea bag and add milk and sugar.
13	Why Is the Boy Sleeping?	causes and effects	• The boy went to bed too late, so he is sleeping in class. • The boy is sleeping in class because he went to bed too late.
14	What Happened?	predictions	• I think some little mice made the shoes. • Maybe someone brought new shoes to help the shoemaker.
15	Let's Tell a Story!	sequences	• First, two boys are playing in the ocean. Then, they see a shark. Next, they get out of the water. Finally, they call out, "Shark!"
16	She Was Mean to Cinderella	opinions on fairy tales	• I agree because the stepmother was so mean to her. • I disagree because she is a good girl.

How to Use This Book

This section is an introduction to the unit and grabs the attention of the students. It has a focus picture followed by three questions. The questions are either comprehension or conversational and are designed to get students talking straight away. Some of the questions act as a springboard to the rest of the unit.

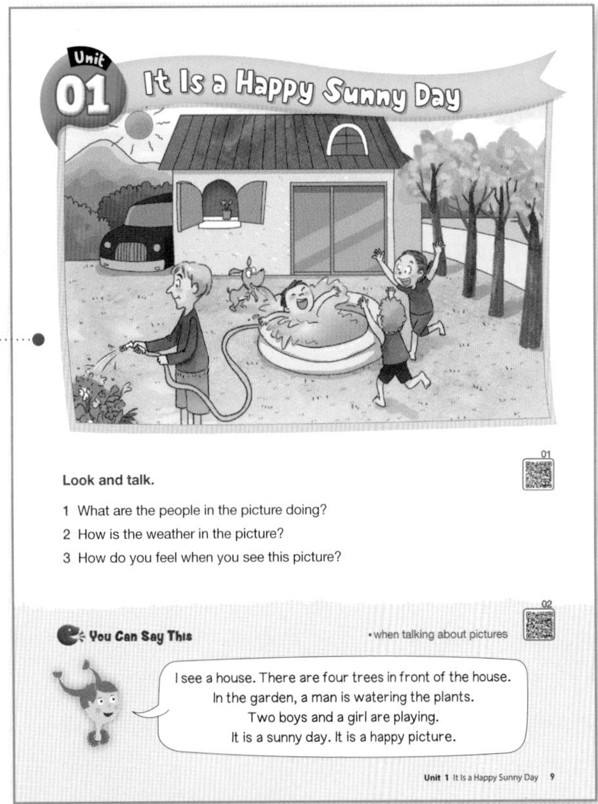

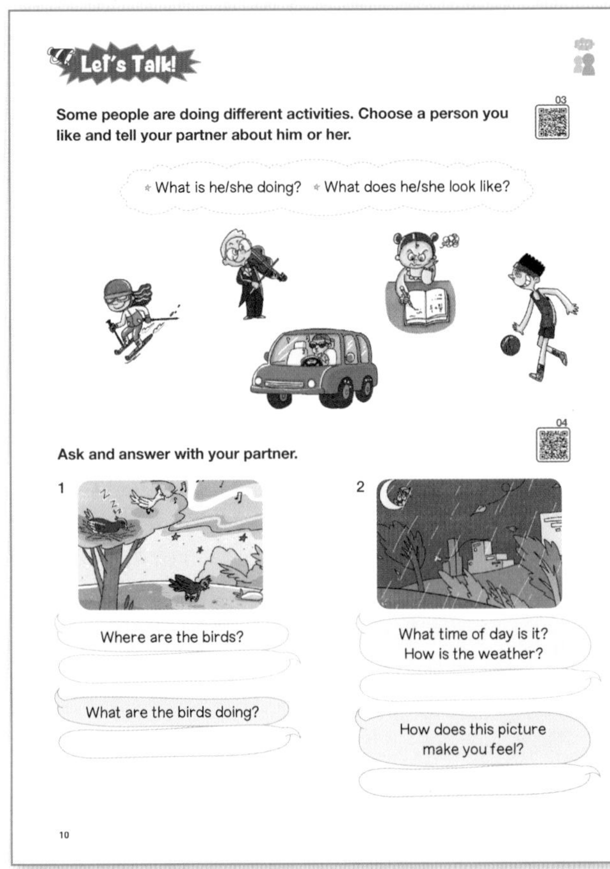

You Can Say This

This part is directly related to some of the questions above. It gives the students key or example phrases and sentences used throughout the unit.

Let's Talk!

This section has two parts. The first part is designed as a conversation. It is a fun way for the students to answer a specific question as they may choose one or two answers from a selection of several choices. The second part allows the students to look at mini pictures and answer questions checking their comprehension and giving them a chance to speak.

Speak Out!

Say what you can see. Then, talk about how you feel about the pictures.

1

2

Unit 1 It Is a Happy Sunny Day 11

Unit 04

Things Around You

Flip a coin and move along the board. When you land on each space, say two things about the object.

+1 +2

Start

24

Unit 01

Spot the Differences

Work in pairs. Find the differences between the two pictures as fast as you can and tell your partner. The winner is the one who finds the most differences.

12

Speak Out!

This section is a group or class activity. It has one question and two large pictures. Each of the pictures has enough material for groups to generate different answers.

Fun Activities

This section allows the students to reinforce or expand their speaking in a fun way. Each unit has activities such as bingo, spot the differences, information gap, find a friend, and a board game. The students can relax and have fun while using English.

☆ **Review Test · Teaching Materials**
free download at www.ihappyhouse.co.kr

TAXI

Unit 01 It Is a Happy Sunny Day

Look and talk.

1 What are the people in the picture doing?

2 How is the weather in the picture?

3 How do you feel when you see this picture?

• when talking about pictures

I see a house. There are four trees in front of the house.
In the garden, a man is watering the plants.
Two boys and a girl are playing.
It is a sunny day. It is a happy picture.

Some people are doing different activities. Choose a person you like and tell your partner about him or her.

03

☆ What is he/she doing? ☆ What does he/she look like?

04

Ask and answer with your partner.

1

Where are the birds?

What are the birds doing?

2

What time of day is it?
How is the weather?

How does this picture make you feel?

Say what you can see. Then, talk about how you feel about the pictures.

1

2

Spot the Differences

Work in pairs. Find the differences between the two pictures as fast as you can and tell your partner. The winner is the one who finds the most differences.

Unit 02 Do Not Touch!

05

Look and talk.

1 Where are the people in the picture?

2 What do the signs mean?

3 Have you seen any of the signs in other places?

06

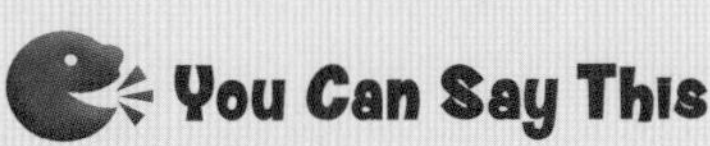

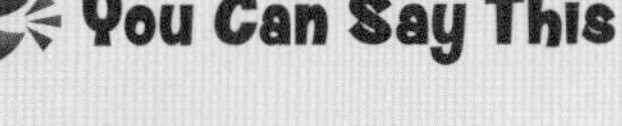

You Can Say This

• when talking about signs and rules

• Do not touch.
• Do not take photos.
• You should not run.
• You should be quiet.

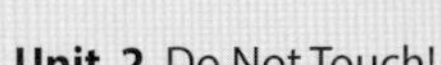

07

Which rules do you like in school? Choose two rules and talk with your partner.

☆ What should we do in school?

08

Ask and answer with your partner.

1

What shouldn't people do when they see this sign?

Where can we see this sign?

2

What does this sign mean?

Where have you seen this sign?

Choose one person and say what he or she is doing wrong. Then, talk about what you would say to him or her.

1

2

Signs Are Everywhere

Flip a coin and move along the board. When you land on each space, say what the sign means.

+1 +2

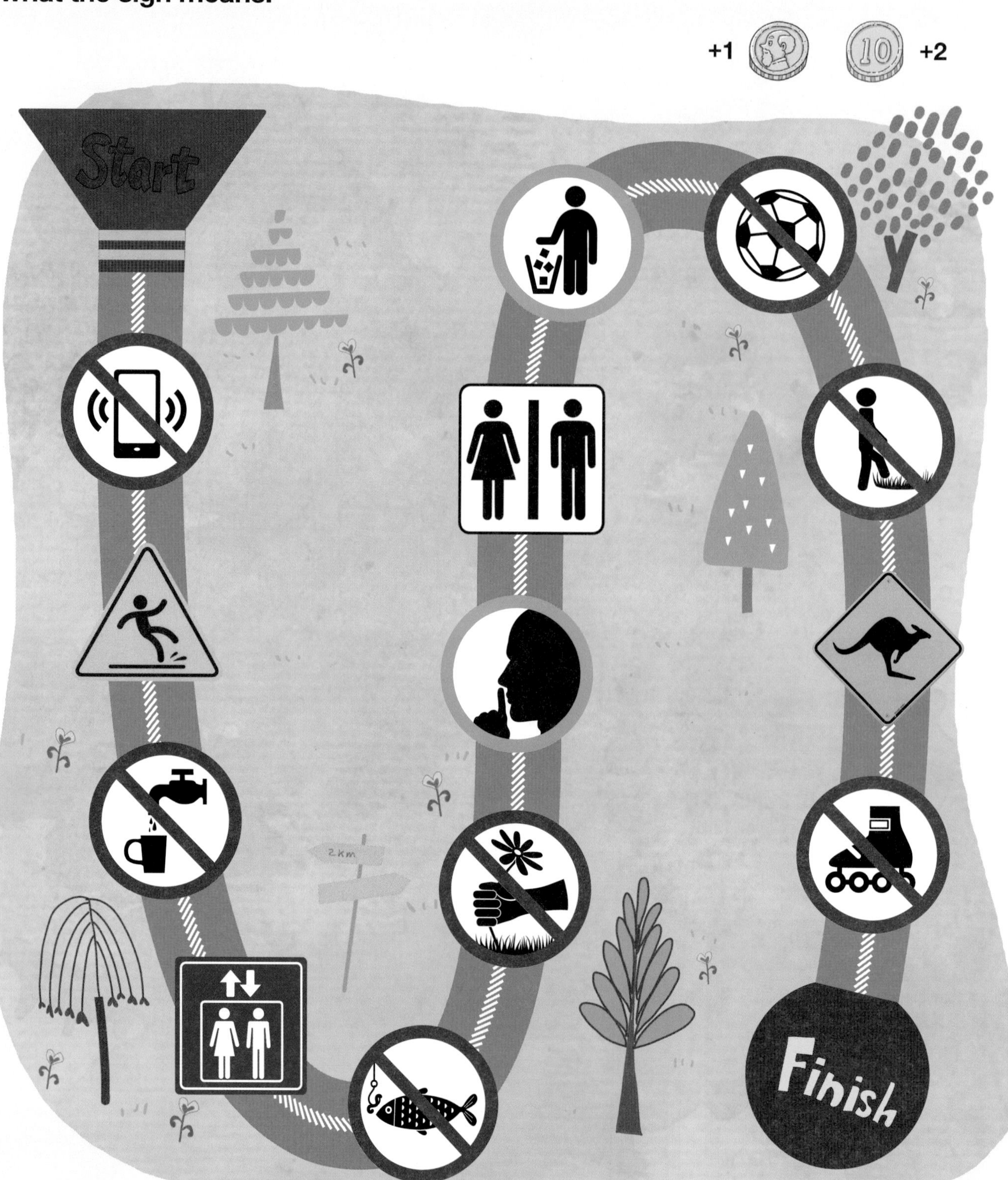

Unit 03

Where Is the Cafeteria?

09

Look and talk.

1 What rooms can you see in the picture?

2 Where is the cafeteria?

3 How can the students get to the cafeteria?

10

• when talking about how to get to a place

The cafeteria is on the third floor.
Go up the stairs. Turn left and go straight.
It is on your left. You can't miss it.

11

You are at a shopping mall. Choose two places you want to visit and ask your partner where they are.

Where is this place?

12

Ask and answer with your partner.

1

What is next to the train station?

How can I get to the post office?

2

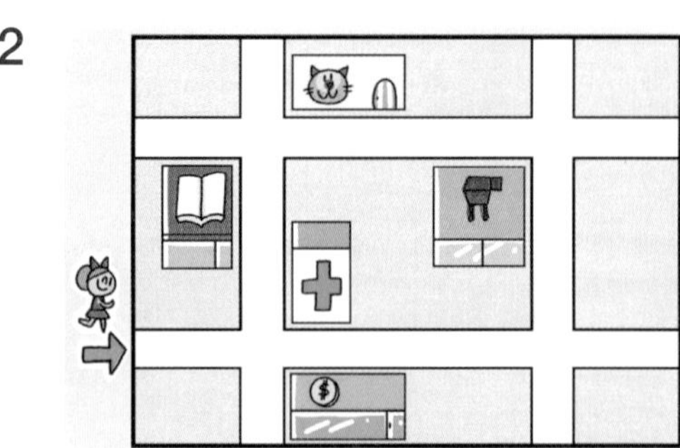

What do you see in the picture?

How can I get to the bookstore?

Choose one place and tell your classmates how to get there. They will guess where you are going.

1

2

Into the Forest Maze

Work in pairs. Choose Little Red Riding Hood or Wolf. Then, take turns giving directions to Grandma's house. The winner is the first one who arrives at Grandma's house.

Unit 04 What Is This For?

13

Look and talk.

1 Where can you find these items?

2 Which one do you write with?

3 What are pencils made of?

14

You Can Say This

• when talking about objects

I draw or write with pencils.
They are long and thin. They are hard.
They are made of wood and lead.
We can see pencils at home, school, and work.

15 

Let's look in the bathroom! Choose an item and ask your partner what he or she uses it to do.

☆ What do you use this for?

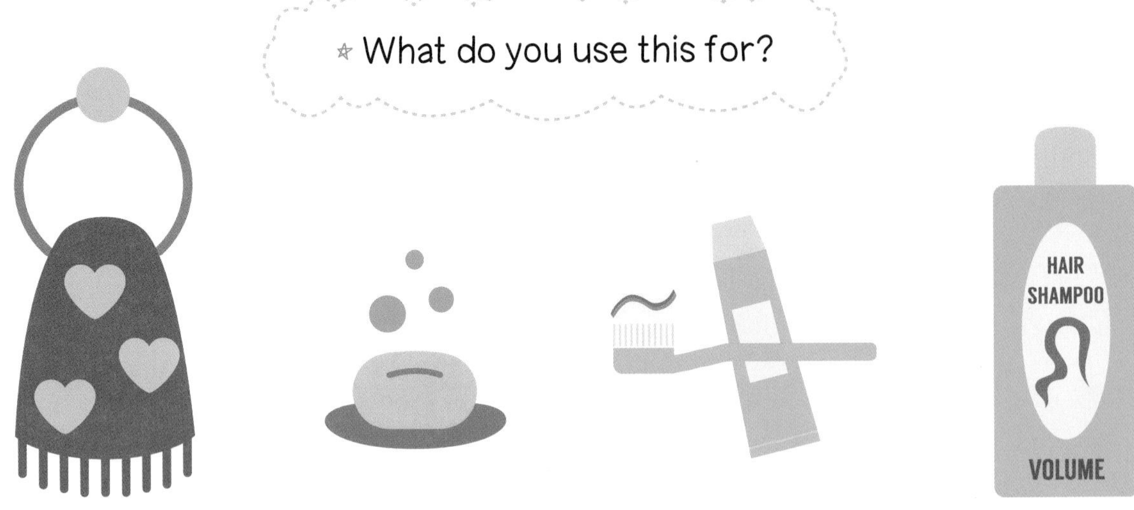

16 

Ask and answer with your partner.

1

What color and shape is the beach ball?

Is it heavy or light?

2

Where can you see these objects?

What are they made of?

Choose one object and say two things about it. Your classmates will guess which object you are talking about.

1

2

Things Around You

Flip a coin and move along the board. When you land on each space, say two things about the object.

+1 +2

Unit 05 They Are Similar but Different

17

Look and talk.

1 What fruits can you see in the picture?

2 What color are they?

3 How do they taste?

• when talking about how things are similar or different

The lemon is yellow. The banana is yellow too.
They are both fruits.
But one is sour and the other is sweet.

19

Let's compare vehicles! Choose two vehicles and ask your partner about how they are different.

☆ How are the vehicles different?

20

Ask and answer with your partner.

1

What is similar about the twin sisters?

What is different about the twin sisters?

2

What are the people doing?

Where are they watching the game?

Choose two animals or flags and say what is similar or different about them.

1

2

How Are They Different?

Work in pairs. Choose a picture and take turns saying one sentence about it. If what your partner says is different from your picture, circle the part. The winner is the first one who has five circles.

Player 1

Player 2

Unit 06

Imagine This!

You can make two wishes.

21

Look and talk.

1 What is happening in the picture?

2 What does the girl want to get?

3 Imagine you have a magic lamp. What would you wish for?

22

• when talking about possible or impossible situations

• I would like superpowers.
• I would wish for a lot of computer games.

23

Imagine a monster is chasing you. Choose what you would do and tell your partner.

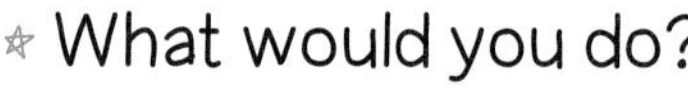

24

Ask and answer with your partner.

1

Why is the toy special?

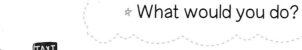

Imagine you have a talking robot. What would you do with it?

2

Imagine you can turn into an animal. Which animal would you choose?

Why did you choose that animal?

Talk about what is happening. Then, imagine you are the boy or girl and talk about what you would do.

1

2

What Would You Do?

Flip a coin and move along the board. When you land on each space, imagine that happens to you and say what you would do.

+1   **+2**

Start

You break your dad's glasses.

You see a spider in your room.

You are lost.

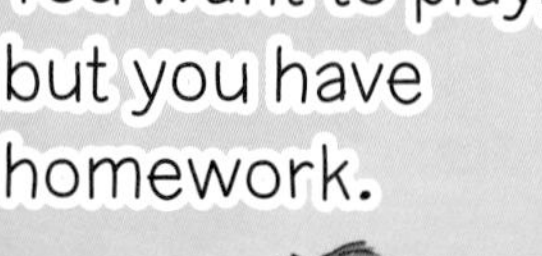

You want to play, but you have homework.

Your tooth falls out at school.

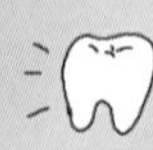

You see a house on fire.

You can't sleep at night.

You get bad grades.

Miss a Turn

Your bag is missing.

You find money on the street.

You don't like fish but your mom cooks fish.

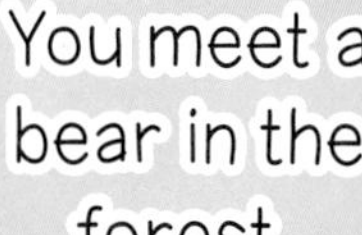

You meet a bear in the forest.

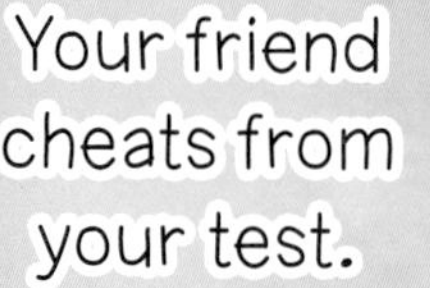

Your friend cheats from your test.

Finish

Unit 07

I Would Rather Choose This

Look and talk.

25

1 What can you see in the picture?

2 Would you rather have only daytime or only nighttime?

3 Imagine there is no more daytime. What would you do?

You Can Say This

• when talking about what you prefer

26

• I would rather have only daytime. I could play all the time.
• I would rather have only nighttime. It would be fun to play in the dark.

27

Your mom asks you to help her with chores. Choose one you would rather do and tell your partner.

28

Ask and answer with your partner.

1

What is happening in the picture?

Would you rather eat carrots or broccoli for one whole day?

2

Would you rather be super smart or super strong?

Would you rather be super strong or super fast?

In the first picture, talk about who you would rather be and what you would do. In the second picture, talk about which time you would rather go to and what you would do.

1

2

Would You Rather

Flip a coin and move along the board. When you land on each space, say what you would rather choose and why.

+1 **+2**

Start

have three eyes or three arms

have no teeth or no hair

be a dad/mom or a child

watch a scary movie or a sad movie

live on the moon or in a jungle

live without a TV or a computer

be a chef or a teacher

live with City Mouse or Country Mouse

have a pet whale or a pet pig

never eat pizza again or never eat chicken again

turn purple or become small when you lie

have a brother or a sister

have a broken arm or a broken leg

Finish

Unit 08 She Needs Some Advice

Look and talk.

1 How does the girl in the picture look?

2 Why do you think she feels that way?

3 She wants to make sure it doesn't happen again. What would you say to her?

• when talking about what to do

• Why don't you hide the bag?
• Why don't you tell your parents about her?
• You should tell her not to take your things.

31

What kinds of problems do you have? Choose and tell your partner.

32

Ask and answer with your partner.

1

What is the girl's problem?

Tell her what she should do.

2

What is the boy's problem?

Tell him what he should do.

Talk about what is happening. Then, talk about what the boy or girl should do.

1

2

What Should I Do?

Flip a coin and move along the board. When you land on each space, give advice to fit the problem.

+1 (coin) (10) +2

Start

I want to lose weight.

I want to speak English well.

I'm always late for school.

My cat is sick.

I get a low score on a science test.

I feel sad.

My parents always read my text messages.

My friend is angry with me.

I'm bored.

I have a toothache.

I'm going to the beach, but I can't swim.

I can't remember what my homework is.

My bedroom is very cold at night.

Finish

Unit 09

What Do You Know about It?

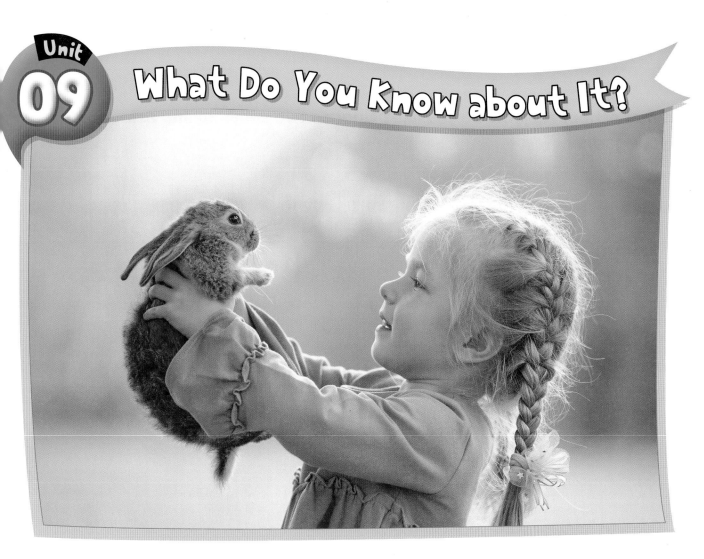

33

Look and talk.

1 What can you see in the picture?

2 What do you know about rabbits?

3 Do you think rabbits are the best animals? If yes, why do you think so?

34

You Can Say This

• when talking about facts and opinions

• Rabbits have a short tail and long ears. They eat carrots.
• I think rabbits are the best animals because they are cute. They are also very quiet.

35

What school subjects do you like? Choose two subjects and ask your partner.

☆ What do you think about this class?

music

English

math

art

science

36

Ask and answer with your partner.

1

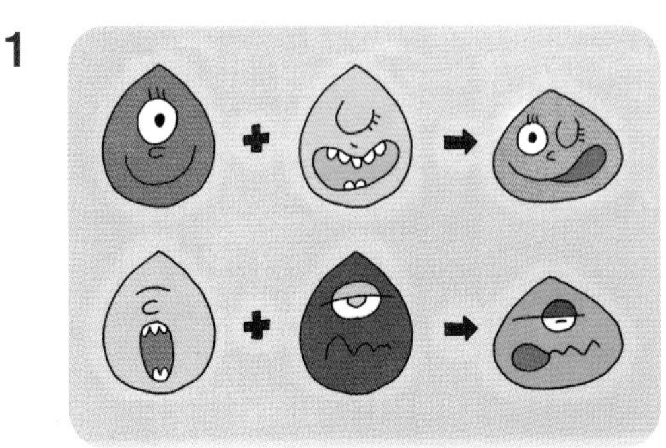

What colors make orange?
What colors make green?

What is your favorite color?
Why do you like it?

2

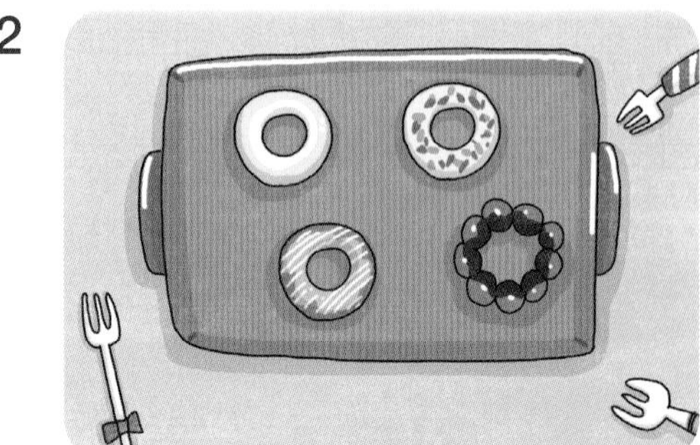

What do these donuts look like?

What do you think about donuts?

Say what you can see. Then, talk about what you think about the pictures.

1

2

Fact and Opinion Bingo

Work in pairs. Take turns saying the number of the picture. When the number is red, say something that is true about it. When the number is green, say what you think about it. Circle the pictures you and your partner say. The winner is the first one who has four circles in a row and calls out, "Bingo!"

Player 1

Player 2 goes to page 86.

Unit 10 This Happened Yesterday

37

Look and talk.

1 What is happening in the picture?

2 What did the boy hurt?

3 Have you ever fallen off your bike? When was it? What happened?

• when talking about what happened in the past (what, when)

38

• I fell off my bike yesterday. I hurt my knee.

• Last weekend, I fell off my bike. I broke my wrist.

39

Sometimes embarrassing things happen. Choose one that happened to you and tell your partner.

☆ Have any of these happened to you? When was it?

40

Ask and answer with your partner.

1

What is happening in the picture?

When you didn't clean your room, what did your mom do?

2

What is happening in the picture?

When your friends wanted to do something you don't like, what did you do?

Talk about what is happening. Then, talk about when that happened to you and what you did at that time.

1

2

What Did You Do?

Flip a coin and move along the board. When you land on each space, say what you did at that time.

+1 +2

Start

when your friend was angry with you

last weekend

when you lost your bag

when you saw a big dog

when you had a bad cold

on your birthday

last Christmas

when you got home yesterday

when you found a wallet on the street

when you met a new friend

when you stayed up late

when you got up this morning

Finish

Unit 11

We Met at the School Yard

Look and talk.

41

1 What is the girl in the picture doing?

2 Do you remember your first day of elementary school? Who did you go with?

3 What did you do on your first day of school?

42

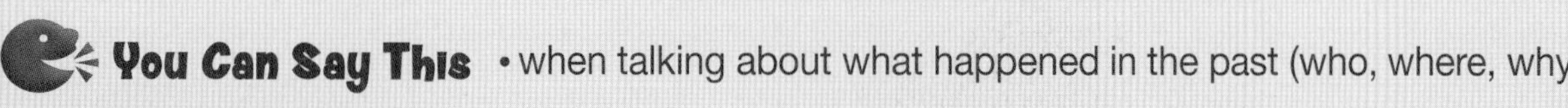

You Can Say This • when talking about what happened in the past (who, where, why)

On my first day of school,
my mom walked with me to school.
I met my classmates at the school yard.
I was nervous because everything was new to me.

43

Have you seen any of these in person? Choose all and tell your partner.

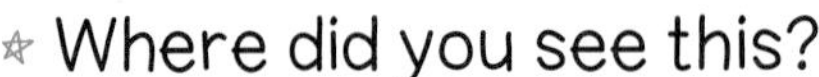

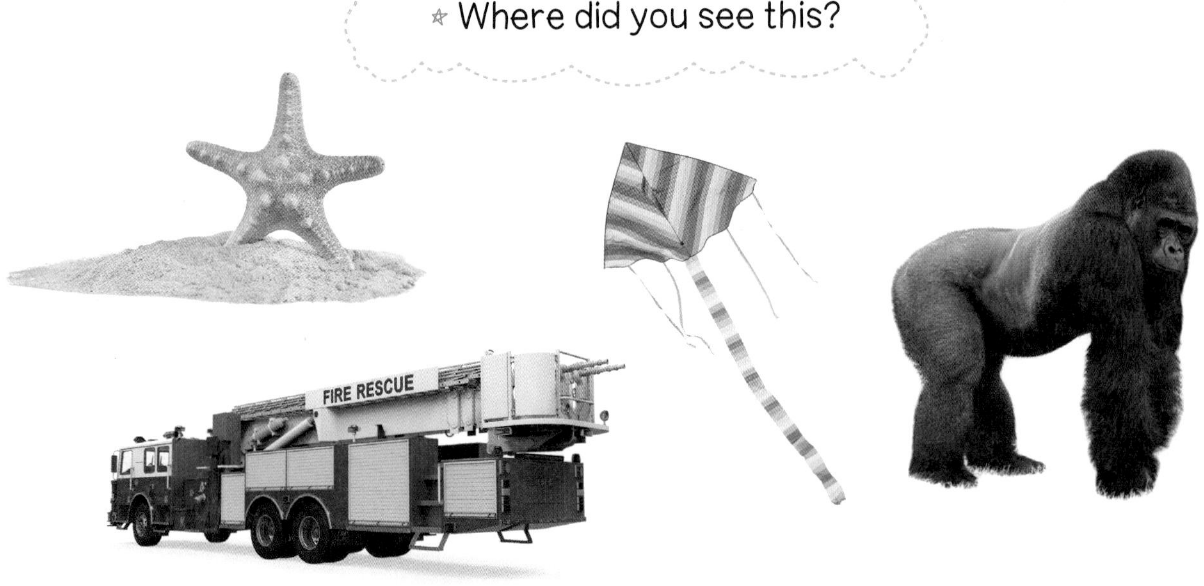

44

Ask and answer with your partner.

1

What is happening in the picture?

Have you had a fight with someone? Who was it?

2

What are the people doing?

Have you gone camping? Why did you like it or not like it?

Choose one item or type of weather and talk about your memories of it.

1

2

Find a Friend!

Ask your classmates if they did these activities last week. If they did, ask him or her to write their last names in the box. The winner is the one who has the most names.

How to play

Q Did you go to a fastfood restaurant last week?

A Yes, I did. ➡ Ask the following question(Who did you go with?).

A No, I didn't. ➡ Ask another classmate.

Did you … last week?

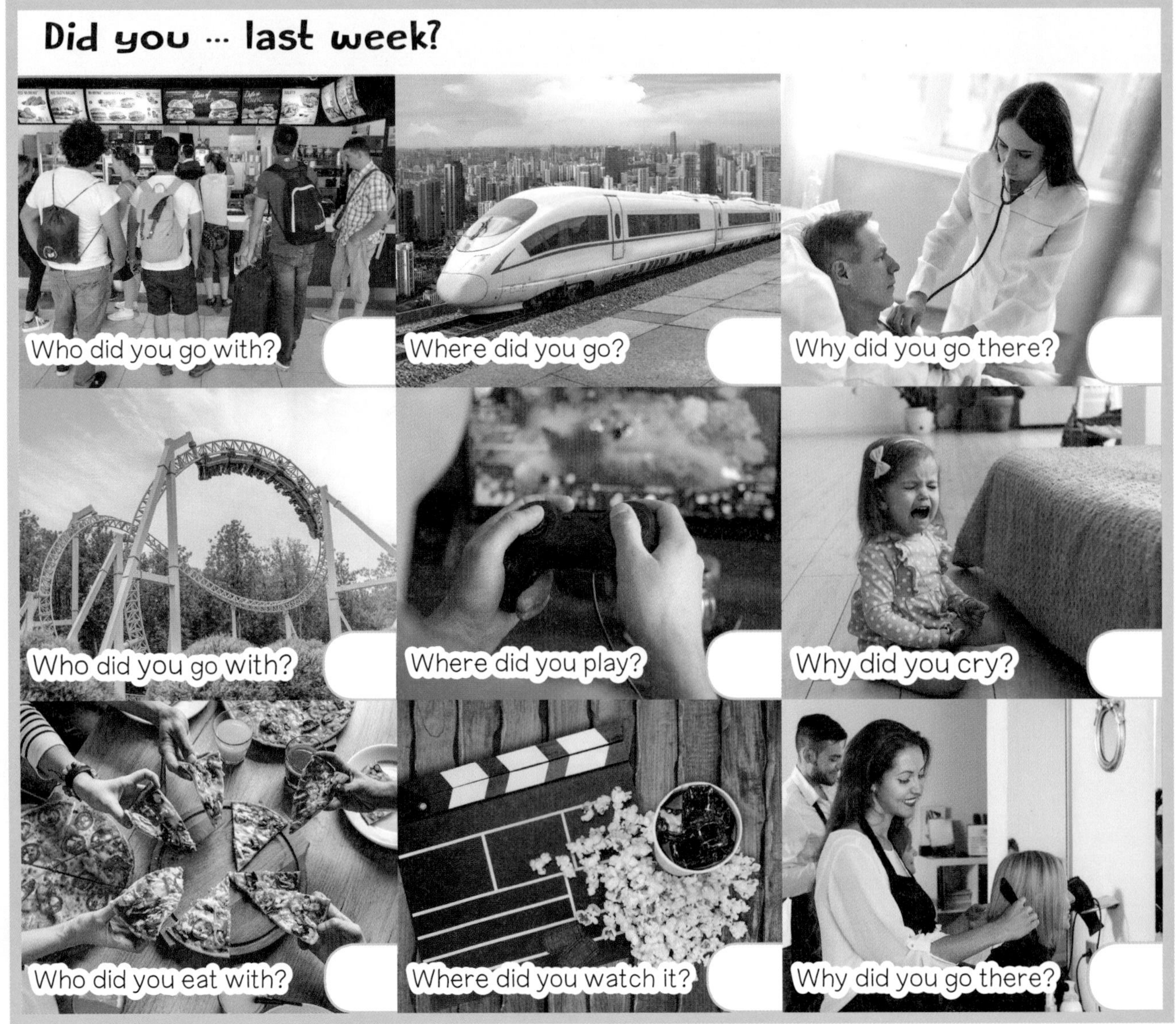

Who did you go with?
Where did you go?
Why did you go there?
Who did you go with?
Where did you play?
Why did you cry?
Who did you eat with?
Where did you watch it?
Why did you go there?

Unit 12 Tell Me How to Make Milk Tea

45

Look and talk.

1 What can you see in the picture?
2 What can you make with these things?

3 Do you know how to make a cup of milk tea?

46

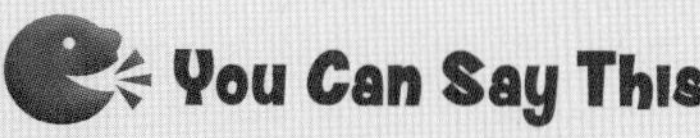

• when talking about how to do something step by step

First, boil the water.
Second, put the tea bag in a cup.
Third, pour the hot water and wait.
Last, remove the tea bag and add milk and sugar.

Let's make the steps to show how to do two simple things!
Choose and ask your partner about the last step.

☆ What is the last thing you do to draw/make this?

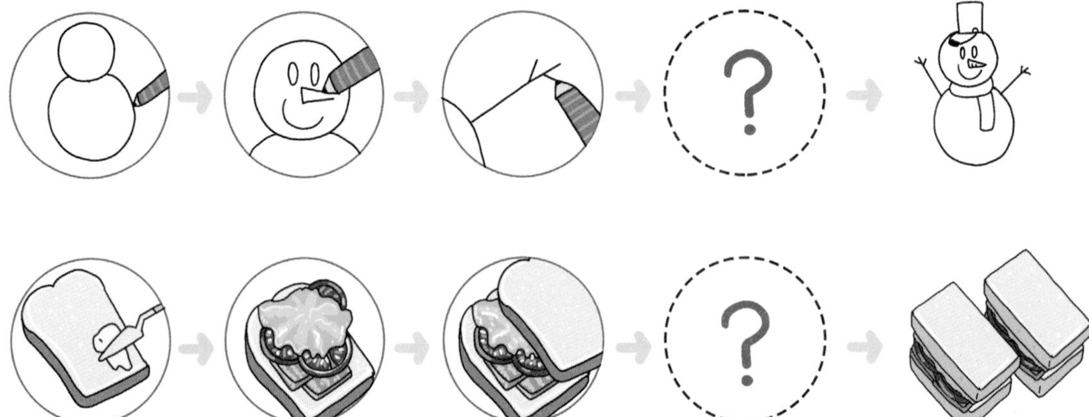

Ask and answer with your partner.

1

What is the boy doing?

How do you get dressed?

2

What is the boy doing?

How do you brush your teeth?

Think about how to make a Christmas card or ramen. Then, say one sentence each in the correct order to make the steps.

1

2

Relay Race

Stand in lines. The person at the front will say the first step for the activity. Then, the next person will repeat what they heard and say the second step. Continue until your line completes all the steps. The winner is the first line that finishes. Take turns and change orders.

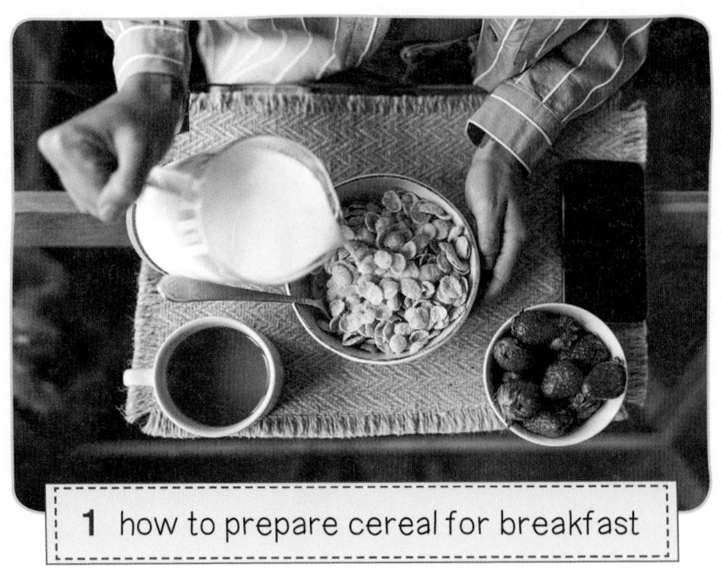

1 how to prepare cereal for breakfast

2 how to boil eggs

3 how to wash your hands

Unit 13

Why Is the Boy Sleeping?

49

Look and talk.

1 What is happening in the pictures?

2 Why is the boy sleeping in class?

3 Have you ever fallen asleep in class? Why?

50

You Can Say This • when talking about why something happens and what happens

- The boy went to bed too late, so he is sleeping in class.
- The boy is sleeping in class because he went to bed too late.

51

These events happen with the weather. Choose and tell your partner about it.

☆ What is happening? ☆ Why is this happening?

52

Ask and answer with your partner.

1

What is happening in the picture?

Why is this happening?

2

What are the baby and the dog doing?

What will happen?

In the first picture, say one sentence each about what is happening and why that is happening. In the second picture, say one sentence each about what happened and what is happening.

1

2

Spot the Differences

Work in pairs. Find the differences between the two pictures as fast as you can and tell your partner the differences in cause and effect. The winner is the one who finds the most differences.

Unit 14

What Happened?

1 2 3 4 5

53

Look and talk.

1 What is happening in the first two pictures?

2 What is happening in the last two pictures?

3 Who do you think made the shoes?

54

• when talking about what you think happened before

• I think some little mice made the shoes.
• I think some elves or fairies made the shoes.
• Maybe someone brought new shoes to help the shoemaker.

The giant is chasing the boy. Choose what you think happened before and talk with your partner.

55

☆ What do you think happened before?

Ask and answer with your partner.

56

1 What is happening in the pictures?

2 What do you think happened in the middle picture?

Look and think about what happened in the middle picture. Then, tell your own story by using the pictures.

What Happened to Them?

Make groups. Read each story and answer the questions together. Then, share the best idea from your group with your classmates.

57

The girl named Little Red Riding Hood liked to visit her grandparents. They lived in an apartment across town. Little Red Riding Hood's mother asked her to take some soup and cake to her grandparents' house. "Please be careful!" her mother said. She was always worried about strangers.
Little Red Riding Hood arrived at her grandparents' house but they did not answer the door. She got in the house, and she was shocked.
A big red monster was there!

1 Why did Little Red Riding Hood visit her grandparents?
2 What did Little Red Riding Hood find at her grandparents' house?
3 What do you think happened to the grandparents?

58

There was a boy named Peter. He always told lies. He lied to his mother and father and everyone!
One day, Peter went to a big store. He said, "Look, there is a thief!" The police came but there was no thief. The next day, he said, "Fire! Fire!" The firemen came, but there was no fire. The next day, Peter lied again. After that Peter did not tell lies anymore. He only told the truth.

1 What did Peter do wrong?
2 What lies did Peter tell?
3 Why do you think Peter stopped telling lies?

Unit 15

Let's Tell a Story!

1 2 3 4

Shark!

59

Look and talk.

1 What is happening in the first two pictures?

2 What do the boys do after they see something in the water?

3 What do the boys do last?

60

• when telling a story in order

First, two boys are playing in the ocean.
Then, they see a shark.
Next, they get out of the water.
Finally, they call out, "Shark!"

61

Brian is fighting with his friend. Choose the reason you think they are fighting and tell your partner.

Why do you think they are fighting?

62

Ask and answer with your partner.

1 Put the numbers in order and tell the story.

2 What do you think the bear said?

Make a story with your classmates by using the pictures. Choose a picture to start the story. Continue until the story is complete.

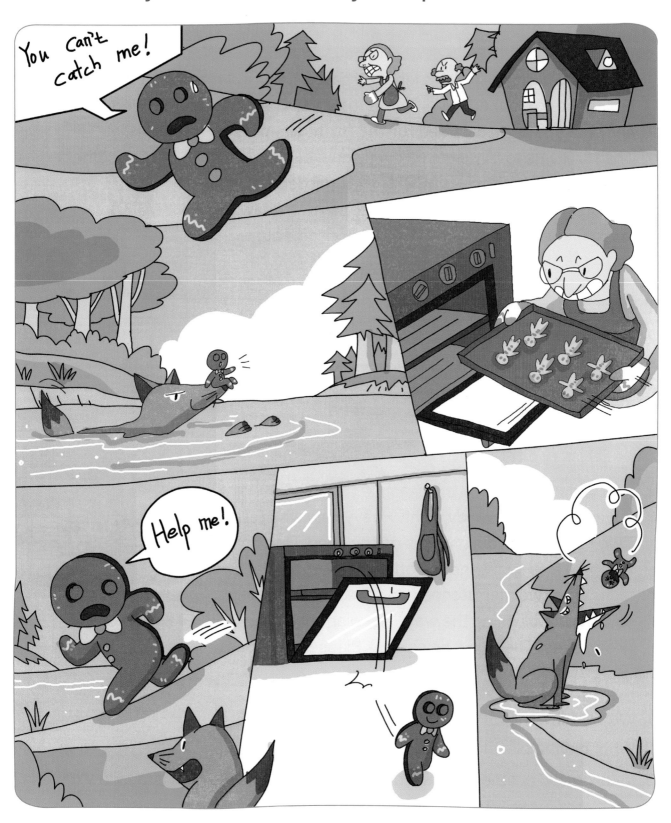

Be the Story Maker!

Make groups. Read each story and answer the questions together. Then, share the best idea from your group with your classmates.

63

Lily was walking in her garden. She saw a beautiful fox beside the rose bush. The fox looked hungry, so she fed it. Then, the fox followed her to her house. She made a bed for the fox to sleep in.
The fox came to Lily's house every day. Lily always gave the fox some delicious food and they walked in her garden.
She and the fox became friends. Lily's friend saw the fox and got jealous. He wanted to be its friend, too.

1 What was the first thing that Lily did to the fox?

2 What did Lily do with the fox every day?

3 Imagine you are Lily's friend. How will you become friends with the fox? Make a plan with three steps.

64

It was a dark and windy night. Heavy rain was falling. Two men were riding horses on the road. One horse was white as snow and the other horse was black as night. The two men stopped on a bridge when they saw a giant blocking the way. The giant had long brown hair and bright green eyes. The two men asked, "Please let us pass."

1 Why did the two men stop on the bridge?

2 What did the giant look like?

3 Imagine you are the giant. What three steps do the men have to follow to pass?

Unit 16 She Was Mean to Cinderella

65

Look and talk.

1 What is Cinderella doing in the first picture?

2 What do you think about Cinderella's stepmother?

3 Do you think Cinderella should punish her stepmother after she marries the prince?

66

• when talking about your opinions

- I agree because the stepmother was so mean to her.
- I disagree because she is a good girl.

What is your favorite fairy tale? Choose and ask your partner if he or she agrees. 67

Ask and answer with your partner. 68

1 What did each of the wolves do wrong?

2 Which wolf is worse?

Tell your partner what you think and ask if he or she agrees.

Say which statement you agree with and why. Write down the names of your classmates who are on the same side as you.

1

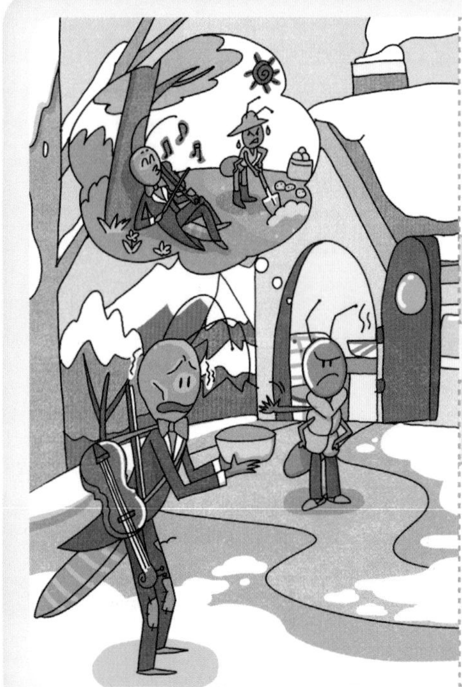

Ant is not kind.

Vs.

Ant is not bad.

2

Country Mouse should live in the city.

Vs.

Country Mouse should go back to the country.

Let's Debate!

Read and debate.

How to debate

1 Read the statement and take a side.
2 Make teams with students who are on the same side.
3 Brainstorm reasons why you agree or disagree. Then, write them down.
4 Now, the debate begins! The two teams take turns saying one reason at a time. The winner is the team that has the most reasons.

Fairy tales are fun to read.

Agree

Disagree

Fairy tales need to have a happy ending.

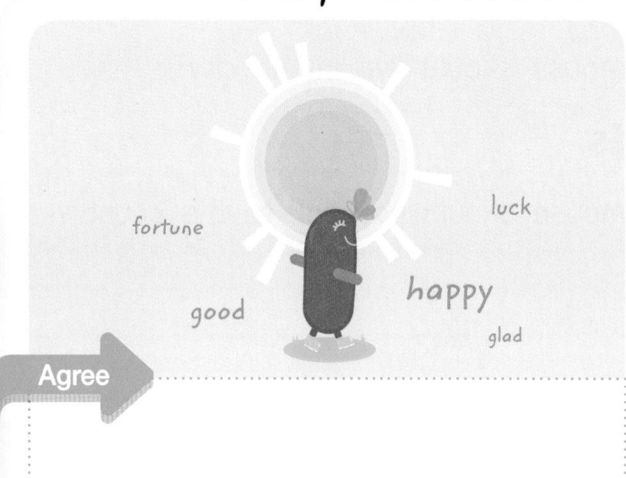

Agree

Disagree

Appendices

Unit 01

sunny

water the plants

ski

play basketball

eat a worm

cross the street

look at his watch

walk her dog

skateboard

sell hot dogs

jump into the pool

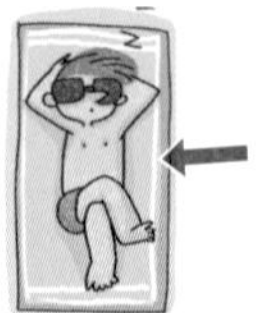
towel

Unit 02

Do not touch.

put trash in the trash can

raise our hand

walk in the hallways

help others

should not smoke

can ride a bike here

eat a hamburger

touch the vase

turn left

drive on a green light

seatbelt

Unit 03

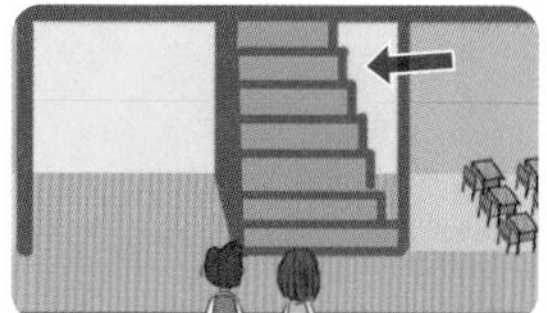
stairs

go straight

turn left

turn right

the first floor

the third floor

the fourth floor

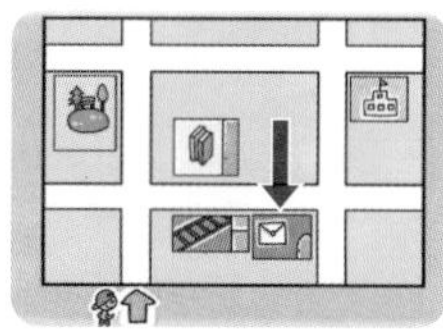
a post office next to the train station

gas station

theme park

a gorilla next to the monkey

crocodile

Unit 04

towel

soap

toothbrush

toothpaste

shampoo

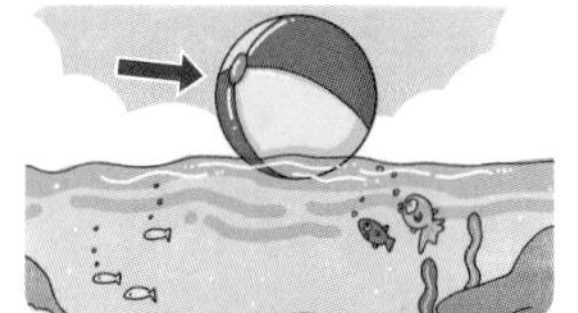
beach ball

orange

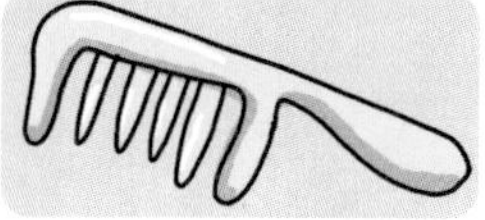
comb

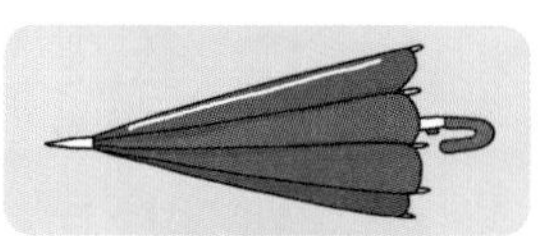
umbrella

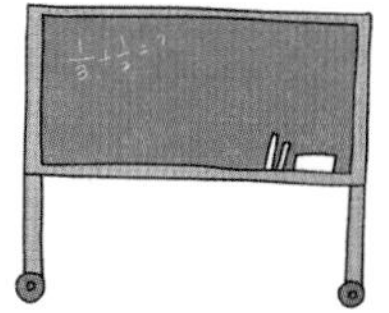
blackboard

mirror

igloo

Unit 05

airplane

ship

bike

wear the same dress

at the stadium

duck

fish

hippo

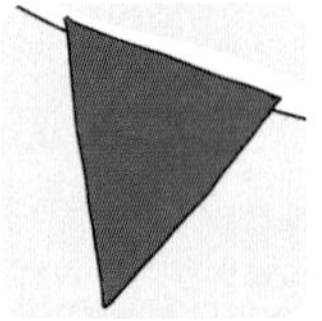
triangle

a green star on it

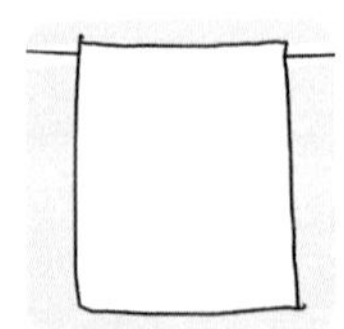
rectangle

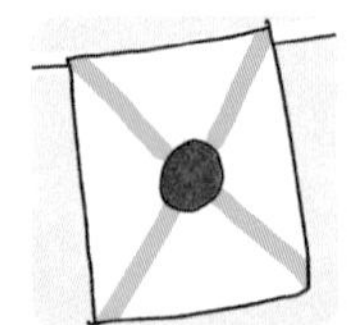
a red circle on it

Unit 06

have a magic lamp

take a taxi

throw my shoe at it

run away

call the police

alone

bully

spider

lost

cheat

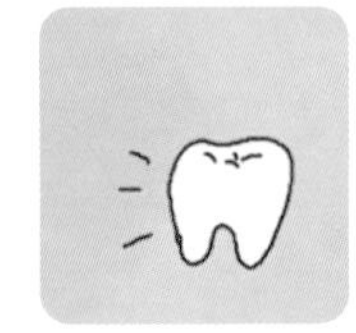
tooth

get bad grades

Unit 07

wash the dishes

clean the house

cook

throw out the trash

do the laundry

broccoli

play basketball

draw a picture

past

dinosaur

future

robot

Unit 08

angry

toothache

like

a bad cold

can't do the math well

fat

can't see the board well

left his wallet on the bus

missing

eat too much chocolate

late for school

sick

Unit 09

fur

music

math

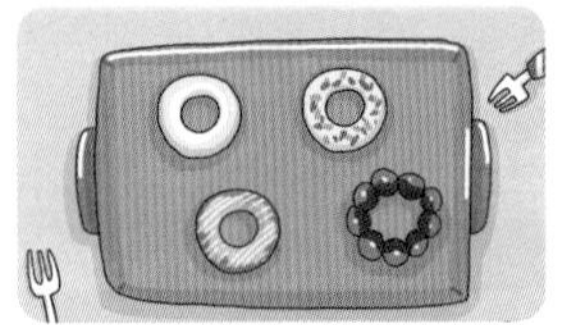
donuts

sunflowers

rainbow

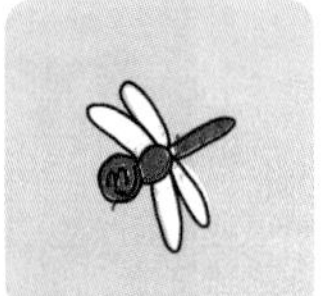
dragonfly

jump

wave her hand

snake

monkey

parrot

Unit 10

hurt

didn't have any money

hole

didn't bring my backpack

There weren't any tissue.

left my umbrella on the bus

messy

go to the movies

cry

home alone

stay up late

get up

Unit 11

starfish

fire engine

kite

gorilla

fight

camp

piano

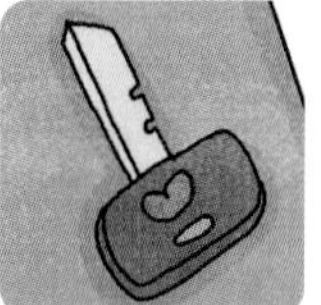
key

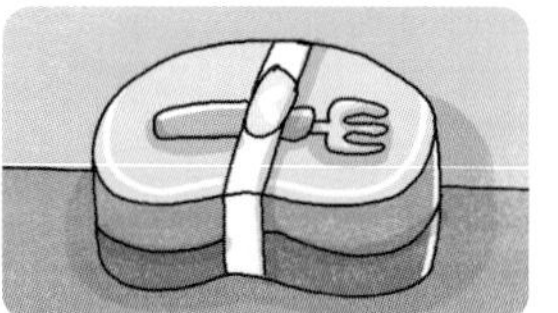
lunch box

windy

thunderstorm

snowy

Unit 12

kettle

tea bag

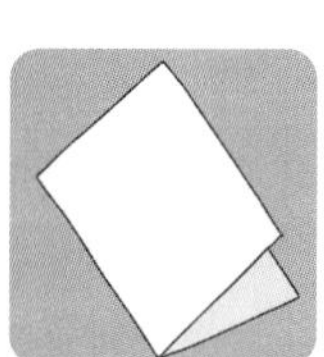
fold

cut out

stick

write

boil water

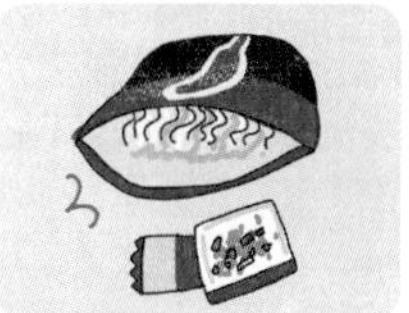
open the ramen noodle packet

put noodles and powder in the water

stir

bowl

cereal

Unit 13

make a snowman

melt

run home in the rain

bark

hot

backpack

enjoy swimming

water park

help her parents

give her money

go to a toy store

sweat

Unit 14

shoemaker

rich

broke the giant's lamp

stole the giant's gold

ate the giant's food

mustache

run away

made of cookies and candies

witch

apartment

worried

thief

Unit 15

shark

get out of the water

cheat

take his friend's snack

tease

break his friend's pencil

go on a picnic

shocked

bake

get out of the oven

cross the river

fox

Unit 16

mean

punish

fairy tales

agree

disagree

grasshopper

ant

work hard

kind

mouse

read

happy ending

Talk Some More 1

**Roll a die and move along the board.
Answer the questions or talk about the pictures.**

Find a person who has a birthday this month.

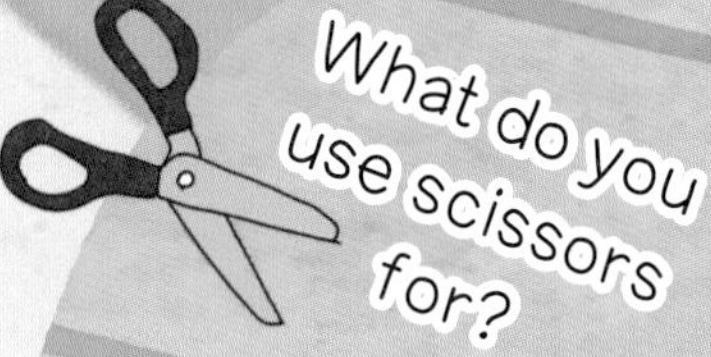

What do you use scissors for?

What is similar about penguins and eagles?

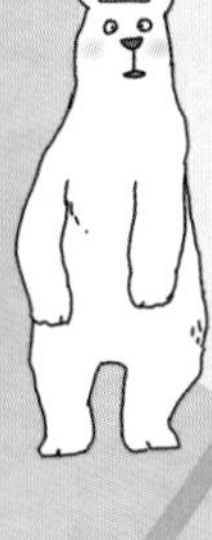

Say something that is true about polar bears.

Have you helped your friend? What did you do?

Name something made of metal.

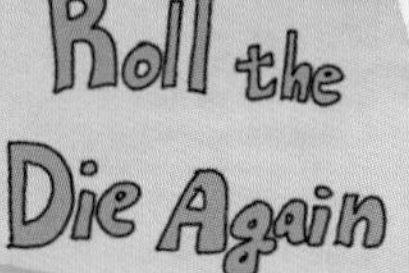

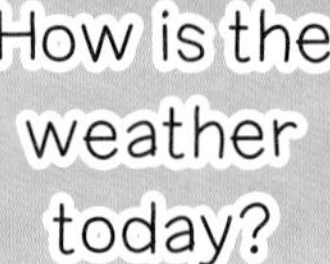

How is the weather today?

I'm tired. What should I do?

What do you think about this hat?

Would you rath
have a pet snak
a pet spider? W

magine you found
n alien in the living
room. What would
you do?

Go Back to Start

Why is the boy crying?

Finish

Have you ever visited another country? Where did you go?

Why is this happening?

How do you wash your hair?

Find a person who read a book yesterday.

Shout "Hello!" Three Times

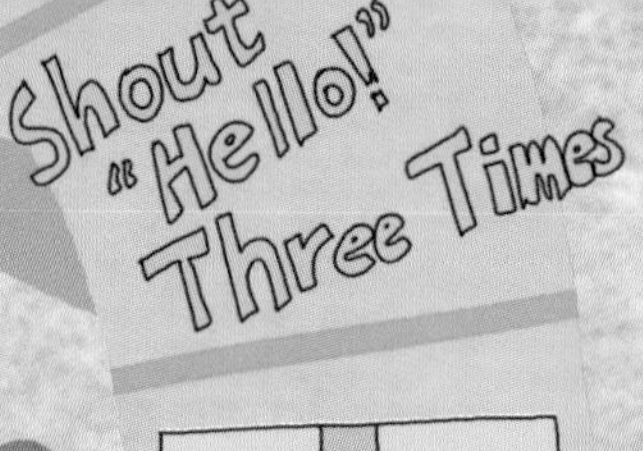

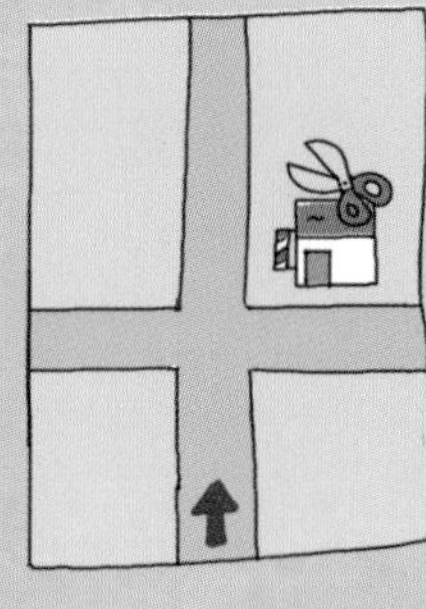

Miss a Turn

When did you watch a movie?

Have you had a fight with someone? Why did you fight?

How can I get to the hair salon?

Talk Some More 2

Roll a die and move along the board.
Answer the questions or talk about the pictures.

When your mom was angry with you, what did you do?

Say something that is true about apples.

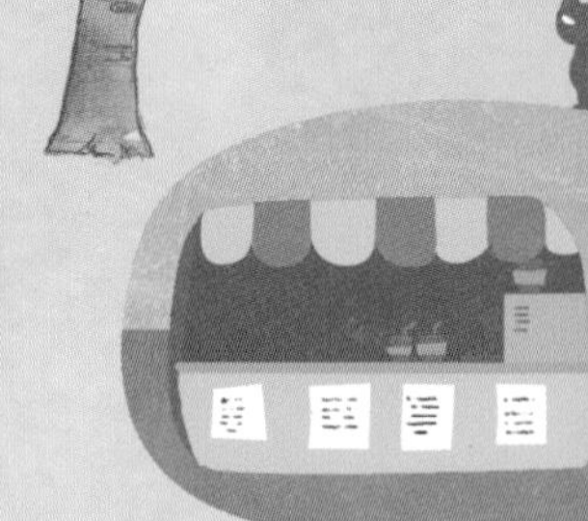

Imagine you turned into your dad. What would you do?

What is different about penguins and eagles?

Why is this happening?

What do you use a chair for?

How do you make a snowman?

Did you talk on the phone yesterday? Who did you talk with?

I'm bored. What should I do?

When did you go to bed last night?

What do you think about your teacher?

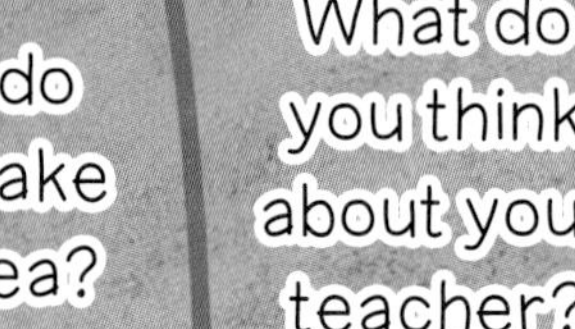

How do you make milk tea?

What do you use a comb for?

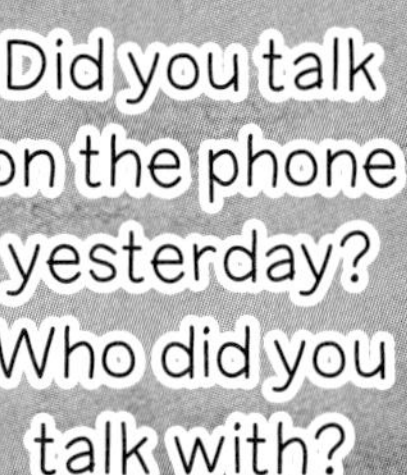

Move Ahead 2 Spaces
Name two things made of wood.
Say what you see and what you think about this picture.
What will happen to him?
Go Back to Start
Should Little Red Hen share the bread with her friends?
Would you rather have a new phone or a new computer? Why?
What do you think about swimming?
Imagine you can be anyone for a day. Who would you be?
Shout "Hurray!" Three Times
Finish

Fact and Opinion Bingo

Work in pairs. Take turns saying the number of the picture. When the number is red, say something that is true about it. When the number is green, say what you think about it. Circle the pictures you and your partner say. The winner is the first one who has four circles in a row and calls out, "Bingo!"

Player 2

Talk
to Me

Talk
to Me

2ND Edition

BUS STOP

Talk to Me

Workbook

2

Happy House

Talk
2ND
Edition
to Me
2
Workbook

Talk to Me 2

2ND Edition

Workbook

Happy House

Picture Description

Picture Discussion

Talk to Me 2

Story Making

Debate

Unit 01

It Is a Happy Sunny Day

A Write the correct words for the pictures.

water the plants	towel	jump into the pool	hot dog	skateboard	sunny

1 

____

2 

____

3 

____

4 

____

5 

____

6 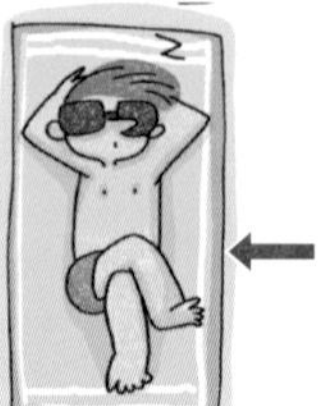

____

B Look and write.

1 

Q What is she doing?

A She is s__________.

2 

Q What does he look like?

A He is t__________. He has short b__________ hair.

C Unscramble and write the sentences.

1 

is eating / The red bird / a worm.

____

2 

It / raining. / is

____

D Complete the sentences using the words in the box.

walking	cap	sunglasses	watch

1 ❶: A boy is crossing the street. He is wearing a purple ____________.

2 ❷: He is looking at his ____________ and walking fast.

3 ❸: A woman is ____________ her dog. She is wearing ____________.

Unit 02 Do Not Touch!

A Write the correct words for the pictures.

seatbelt	turn left	raise	help others	listen to the teacher	swim

1 

____

2 

____

3 

____

4 

____

5 

____

6 

____

B Look and write.

1 

Q What should we do in school?

A We should put t__________ in the t__________ can.

2 

Q What should we do in school?

A We should w__________ in the hallways.

C Unscramble and write the sentences.

1 

You / smoke. / should not

____

2 

can ride / You / a bike / here.

____

D Look and write T for true or F for false.

1 ❶: The girl is eating a hamburger. (   )

2 ❷: The boy is taking a picture. (   )

3 ❸: The girl is touching a book. (   )

Unit 03 Where Is the Cafeteria?

A Write the correct words for the pictures.

go straight	turn left	turn right	gas station	theme park	crocodile

1 
____

2 
____

3 
____

4 
____

5 
____

6 
____

B Look and write.

1 

Q What is next to the train station?

A There is a p__________ o__________ next to the train station.

2 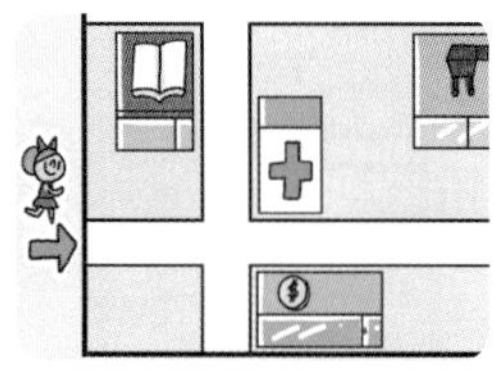

Q How can I get to the bookstore?

A Go straight. Turn l__________ and go straight. It is on your l__________.

C Unscramble and write the sentences.

1 is / The supermarket / on the first floor.

____

2 next to the bakery. / The toy store / is

____

D Complete the sentences using the words in the box.

right straight left

1 If you want to go to the giraffe, turn left and go ______________.

Turn right. Go straight one block. It is on your ______________.

2 If you want to go to the lion, turn ______________ and go straight.

It is on your left.

Unit 04 What Is This For?

A Write the correct words for the pictures.

shampoo   blackboard   toothbrush   mirror   toothpaste   igloo

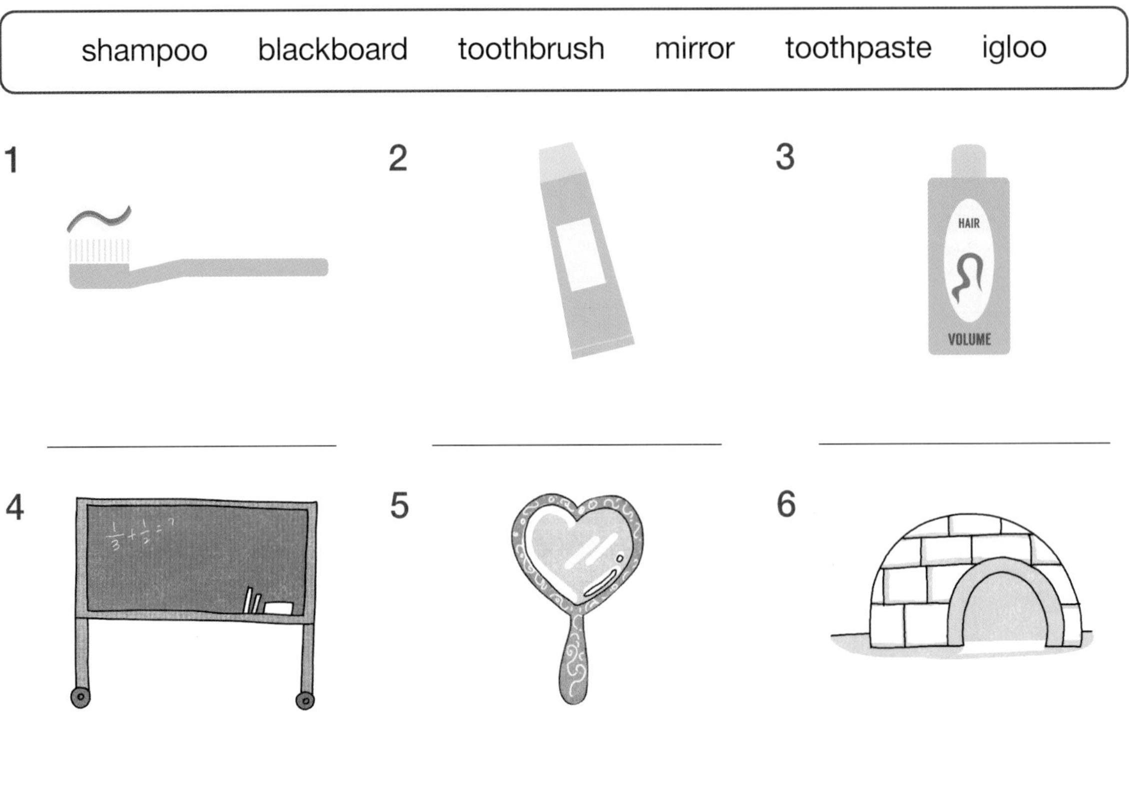

1 ____________

2 ____________

3 ____________

4 ____________

5 ____________

6 ____________

B Look and write.

1

Q What do you use this for?

A I use a t__________ to dry my hair and face.

2

Q What do you use this for?

A I use s__________ to wash my hands and body.

C Read and match.

What are pencils made of? •

What color and shape is the beach ball? •

• They are made of wood and lead.

• It is red, yellow, and green. It is round.

D Look and write T for true or F for false.

1 ❶ orange: This is rectangle. It tastes sour and sweet. ( )

2 ❷ comb: This is yellow. I use it to brush my hair. ( )

3 ❸ umbrella: This is long and purple. I use it on a sunny day. ( )

Unit 05 They Are Similar but Different

A Write the correct words for the pictures.

duck fish hippo rectangle lizard at home

1 
____

2 
____

3 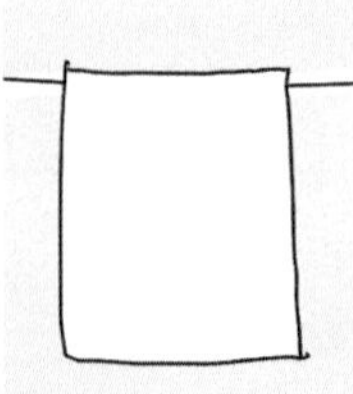
____

4 
____

5 
____

6 
____

B Look and write.

1 

Q How are the vehicles different?

A An a__________ flies in the sky.

A s__________ moves on the sea.

2 

Q What is similar about the twin sisters?

A They are wearing the same d__________.

They both are wearing g__________.

C Unscramble and write the sentences.

1

moves / A bike / on the road.

____

2

The girl / the game / is watching / at the stadium.

____

D Complete the sentences using the words in the box.

circle	triangle	star	heart

1 ❶: It is a ______________. It has a white ______________ on it.

2 ❷: It is a triangle. It is white. It has a green ______________ on it.

3 ❸: It is a rectangle. It is white and blue. It has a red ______________ on it.

Unit 06 Imagine This!

A Write the correct words for the pictures.

get bad grades	alone	call the police	cheat	spider	tooth

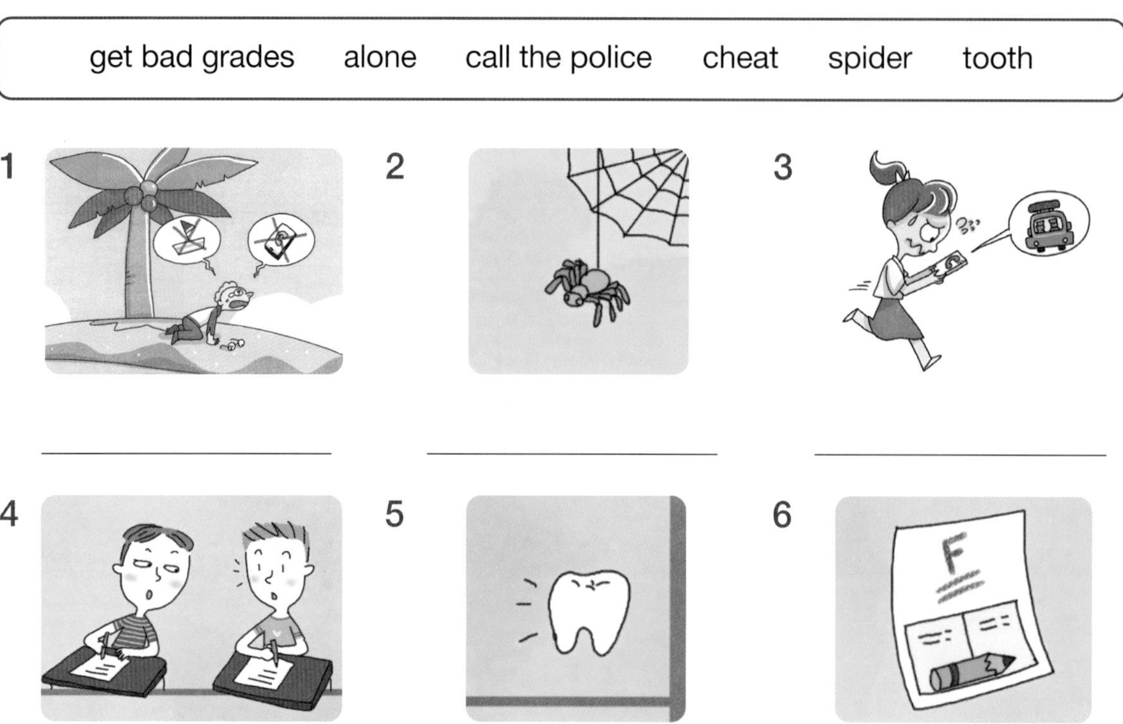

1 ______________ 2 ______________ 3 ______________

4 ______________ 5 ______________ 6 ______________

B Look and write.

1

Q Imagine a monster is chasing you. What would you do?

A I would take a t__________.

2

Q Imagine a monster is chasing you. What would you do?

A I would r__________ away.

C Read and match.

Imagine you can turn into an animal. Which animal would you choose? •	• I would wish for a lot of computer games.
Imagine you have a magic lamp. What would you wish for? •	• I would tell the robot my secrets.
Imagine you have a talking robot. What would you do with it? •	• I would choose a rabbit.

D Look and write T for true or F for false.

1 A big boy is helping another boy. (   )

2 A girl is going home and sees them. (   )

Unit 07 I Would Rather Choose This

A Write the correct words for the pictures.

play basketball	draw a picture	wash the dishes	watch TV	cook	future

1  ____________

2  ____________

3  ____________

4  ____________

5  ____________

6  ____________

B Look and write.

1 

Q What would you rather do?

A I would rather do the l__________.

2 

Q What would you rather do?

A I would rather throw o__________ the trash.

C Unscramble and write the sentences.

1 

The girl / carrots and broccoli. / has

____

2 

I / clean / would rather / the house.

____

D Complete the sentences using the words in the box.

robots	past	dinosaurs	would rather

1 ❶: I would rather go to the ______________.

I would see the ______________ and take a picture with them.

2 ❷: I ______________ go to the future. In the future, ______________

would do my homework and clean my room.

Unit 08

She Needs Some Advice

A Write the correct words for the pictures.

fat   late for school   angry   sick   like   toothache

1 
____

2 
____

3 
____

4 
____

5 
____

6 
____

B Look and write.

1 

A Tell her what she should do.

B You should wear g__________.

2 

A Tell him what he should do.

B You should call the b__________ company.

C Read and match.

What is your problem? •		• You should tell her not to take your things.
She wants to make sure it doesn't happen again. What would you say to her? •		• I have a bad cold.

D Look and write T for true or F for false.

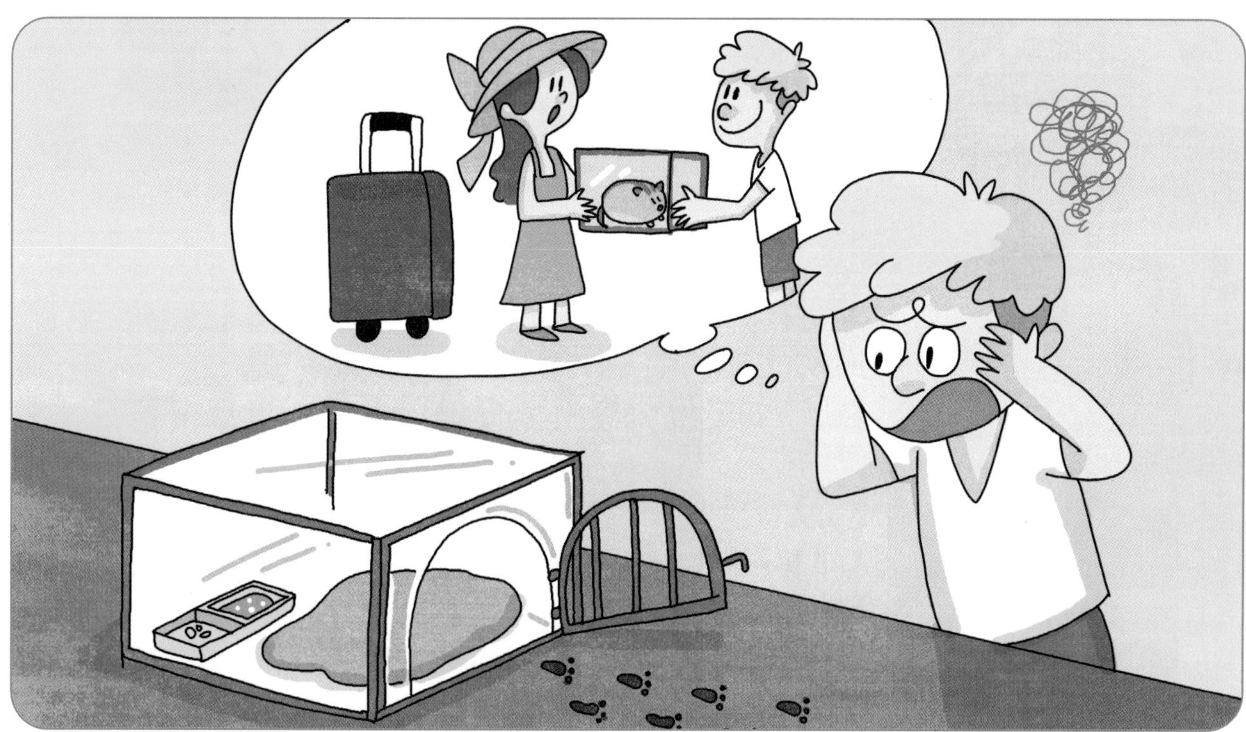

1 His friend left him a hamster. (   )

2 His friend's hamster is in the cage now. (   )

3 He should look for the hamster with other friends. (   )

Unit 09 What Do You Know about It?

A Write the correct words for the pictures.

science sunflowers dragonfly jump rainbow umbrella

1 

____

2 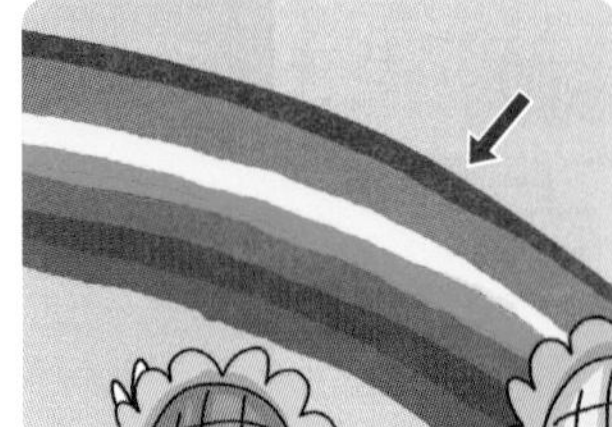

____

3 

____

4 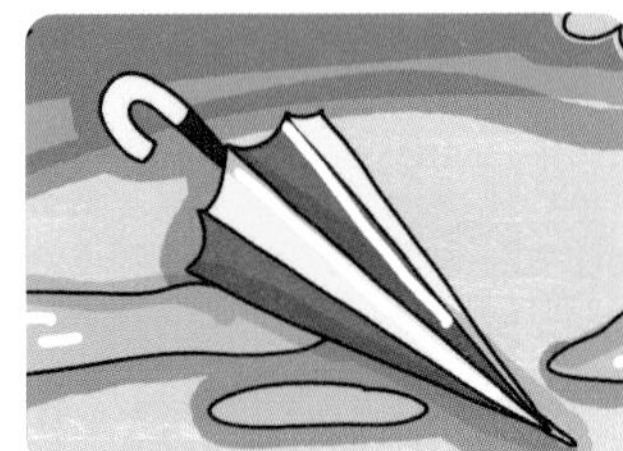

____

5 

____

6 

____

B Look and write.

1 

Q What do you think about this class?

A I think m__________ class is fun.

2 

Q What do you think about this class?

A I think m__________ class is boring.

C Unscramble and write the sentences.

1 

a short tail / Rabbits / and / have / long ears.

____

2 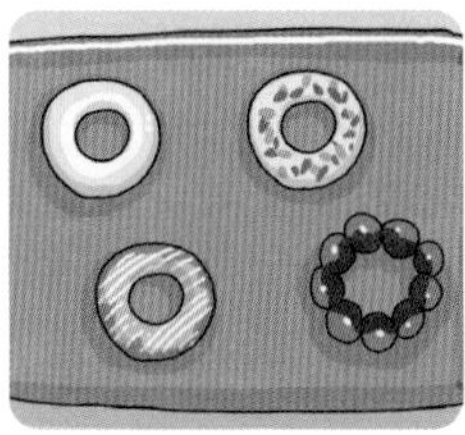

circles. / look like / Donuts

____

D Complete the sentences using the words in the box.

snake	parrot	waving

1 The girl is ______________ her hand.

2 There is a ______________ and a monkey in the trees.

3 There is a ______________ on top of the bus.

Unit 10 This Happened Yesterday

A Write the correct words for the pictures.

home alone	hurt	go to the movies	hole	messy	stay up late

1 

____

2 

____

3 

____

4 

____

5 

____

6 

____

B Look and write.

1 

Q What happened?

A I went to a supermarket last week.

But I didn't have any m__________.

2 

Q What happened?

A Last Friday, I didn't bring my b__________ to school.

C Read and match.

When you didn't clean your room, what did your mom do? •

When your friends wanted to do something you don't like, what did you do? •

• She shouted, "Clean your room right now!"

• I said "No!" and went home.

D Look and write T for true or F for false.

1 The boy had a bad dream. (   )

2 There was a monster in his dream. (   )

3 He is happy. (   )

We Met at the School Yard

A Write the correct words for the pictures.

windy snowy thunderstorm gorilla kite camp

1 ______________ 2 ______________ 3 ______________

4 ______________ 5 ______________ 6 ______________

B Look and write.

1

Q Where did you see this?

A I saw a s__________ at the beach.

2

Q Where did you see this?

A I saw a f__________ e__________ on the road.

C Unscramble and write the sentences.

1 

at the school yard. / met / I / my classmates

____

2 

The children / for the TV remote. / are fighting

____

D Match the pictures with the correct sentences.

1  • • Last weekend, I met my teacher on the bus.

2  • • My dad bought me a piano last Christmas.

3  • • I lost my house key last week.

4  • • I bought a new lunch box.

Unit 12 Tell Me How to Make Milk Tea

A Write the correct words for the pictures.

write	tea bag	fold	kettle	cut out	stick

1 
____

2 
____

3 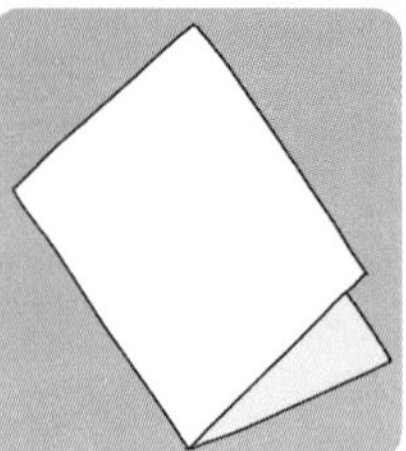
____

4 
____

5 
____

6 

____

B Look and write.

1 Q What is the last thing you do to draw this?

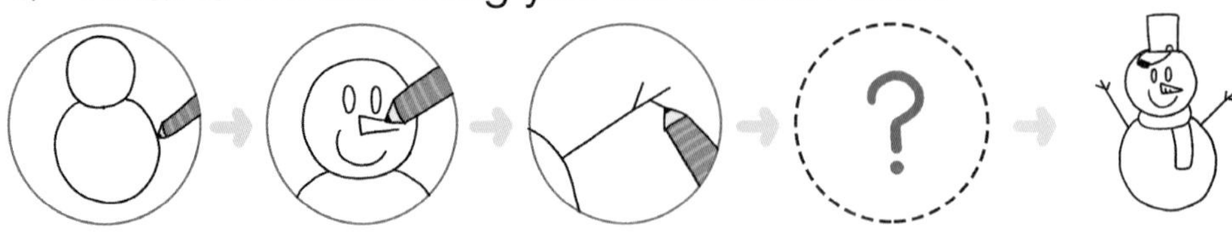

A Last, draw a hat and a s__________.

2 Q What is the last thing you do to make this?

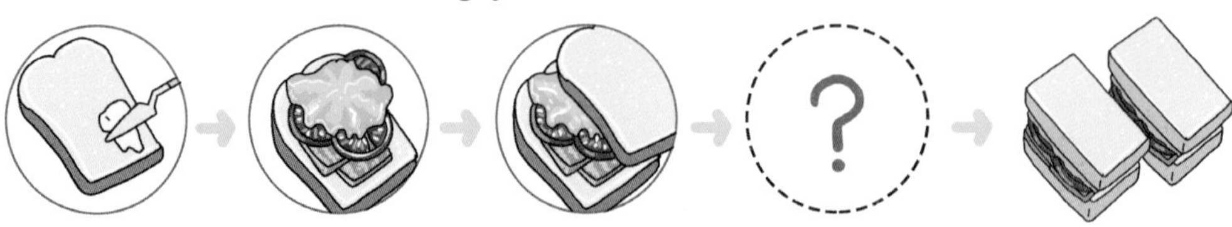

A Last, c__________ the sandwich.

C Read and match.

What can you make with these things? •

What is the boy doing? •

• He is looking at his clothes.

• I can make milk tea.

D Look and write T for true or F for false.

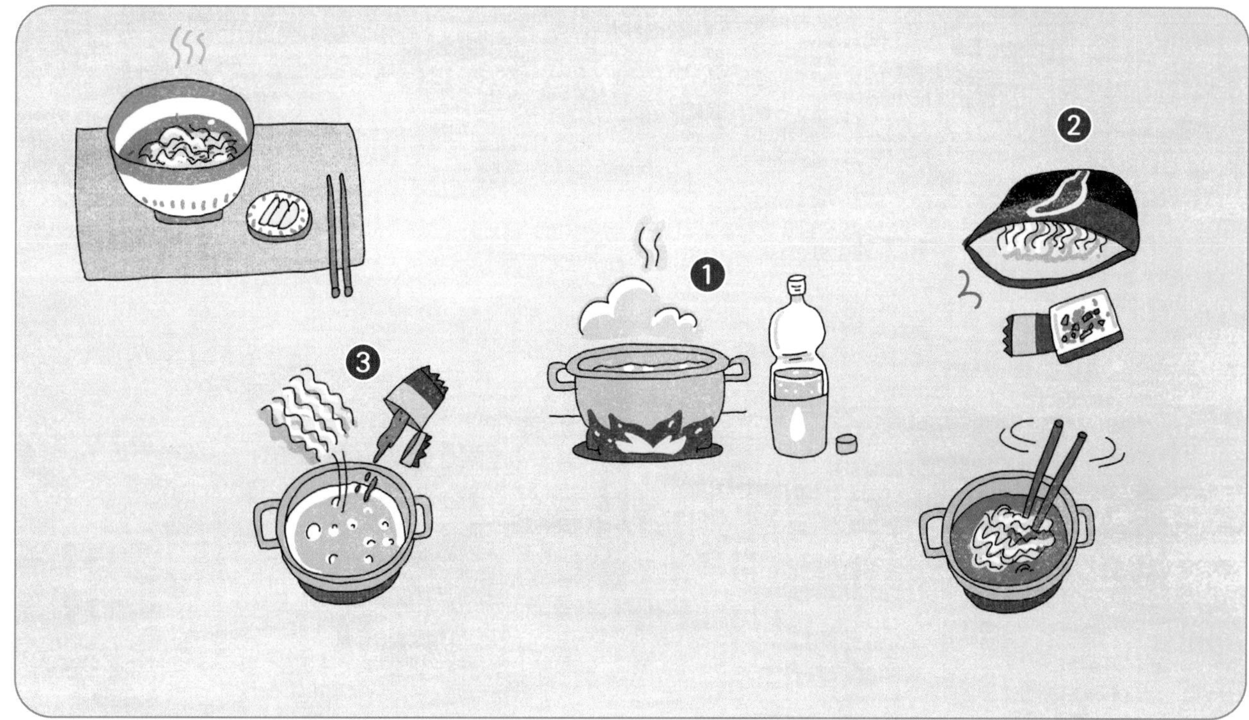

1 ❶: First, boil water in a pot. (   )

2 ❷: Second, close the ramen noodle packet. (   )

3 ❸: Third, put the noodles and powder in the water. (   )

Unit 13

Why Is the Boy Sleeping?

A Write the correct words for the pictures.

enjoy swimming   hot   laugh   sweat   water park   bark

1 
____

2 
____

3 
____

4 
____

5 
____

6 
____

B Look and write.

1 

Q What is happening?

A A boy is making a s__________.

2 

Q Why is this happening?

A Because it is h__________.

C Unscramble and write the sentences.

1 

The boy / in class. / is sleeping

____

2 

is running home / The boy / in the rain.

____

D Complete the sentences using the words in the box.

give toy helps

1 ❶: A girl ______________ her parents.

2 ❷: Her parents ______________ her some money.

3 ❸: She goes to a ______________ store.

Unit 14

What Happened?

A Write the correct words for the pictures.

mustache   apartment   thief   shoemaker   rich   witch

1 

____

2 

____

3 

____

4 

____

5 

____

6 

____

B Match the pictures with the correct sentences.

1  •   • I think the boy ate the giant's food.

2  •   • I think the boy broke the giant's lamp.

3  •   • Maybe the boy stole the giant's gold.

C Match the number in the picture to the correct sentence.

1 ________ They buy a pizza.

2 ________ They go into the house and see a witch there.

3 ________ Then they go back home and see a special house.
It is made of cookies and candies.

4 ________ A boy and a girl go to buy pizza.

D Look and write.

asked	shocked	strangers	visit

The girl named Little Red Riding Hood liked to ________ her grandparents. They lived in an apartment across town. Little Red Riding Hood's mother ________ her to take some soup and cake to her grandparents' house. "Please be careful!" her mother said. She was always worried about ________. Little Red Riding Hood arrived at her grandparents' house but they did not answer the door. She got in the house, and she was ________. A big red monster was there!

Unit 15 Let's Tell a Story!

A Write the correct words for the pictures.

shocked	go on a picnic	break	shark	fox	get out of the water

1  ____________

2  ____________

3  ____________

4  ____________

5  ____________

6  ____________

B Match the pictures with the correct sentences.

1 

• • I think Brian cheated on his test.

2  • • Maybe Brian teased his friend.

3  • • I think Brian took his friend's snack.

C Match the number in the picture to the correct sentence.

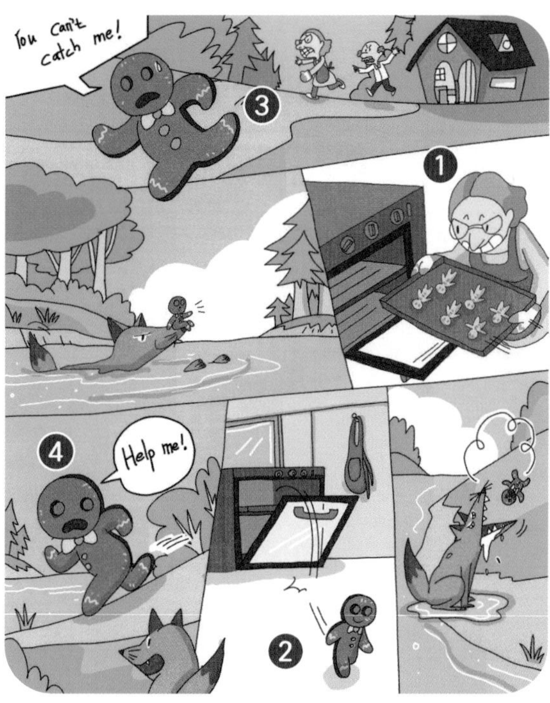

1 ________ The grandfather and grandmother try to catch the cookie.

2 ________ One of the cookies gets out of the oven.

3 ________ The cookie meets a fox at the river. It says "Help me!" to the fox.

4 ________ The grandmother bakes cookies.

D Look and write.

night riding pass saw

It was a dark and windy night. Heavy rain was falling.
Two men were ________ horses on the road. One horse was white as snow and the other horse was black as ________. The two men stopped on a bridge when they ________ a giant blocking the way.
The giant had long brown hair and bright green eyes. The two men asked, "Please let us ________."

Unit 16 She Was Mean to Cinderella

A Write the correct words for the pictures.

kind	grasshopper	ant	fairy tales	agree	disagree

1 Pinocchio Sleeping Beauty ____________

2 ____________

3 ____________

4 ____________

5 ____________

6 ____________

B Look and write.

1 

Q Do you think Cinderella should punish her stepmother after she marries the prince?

A I d__________ because she is a good girl.

2 

Q Do you think Cinderella should punish her stepmother after she marries the prince?

A I a__________ because the stepmother was so mean to her.

C Unscramble and write the sentences.

1 

The best fairy tale / *Alice in Wonderland*. / is

____

2 

Country Mouse / in the city. / should live

____

D Complete the sentences using the words in the box.

because grandmother broke

1 The wolf on the left ate the ______________.

2 The wolf on the right ______________ the pigs' houses.

3 I think the wolf on the right is worse ______________ the poor pigs don't have homes now.

Key Sentences Review

Look and write.

1 (1)

Q What is she doing?

A She is s_________.

(2)

Q What does he look like?

A He is t_________. He has short b_________ hair.

2 (1)

Q What should we do in school?

A We should put t_________ in the t_________ can.

(2)

Q What should we do in school?

A We should w_________ in the hallways.

3 (1)

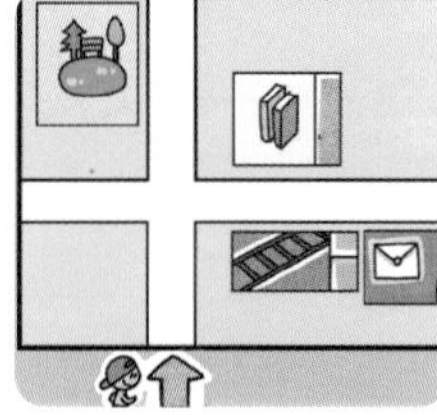

Q What is next to the train station?

A There is a p_________ o_________ next to the train station.

(2)

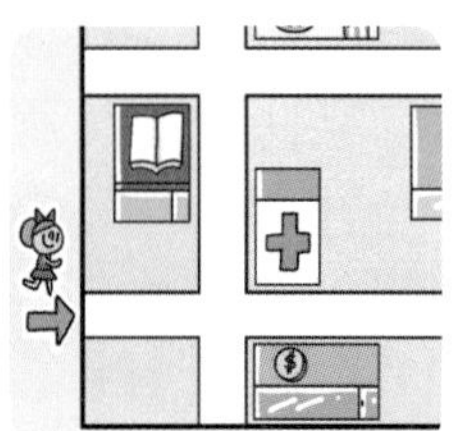

Q How can I get to the bookstore?

A Go straight. Turn l_________ and go straight. It is on your l_________.

4 (1)

Q What do you use this for?

A I use a t_________ to dry my hair and face.

(2)

Q What do you use this for?

A I use s_________ to wash my hands and body.

5 (1)

Q How are the vehicles different?

A An a_________ flies in the sky.

A s_________ moves on the sea.

(2)

Q What is similar about the twin sisters?

A They are wearing the same d_________.

They both are wearing g_________.

6 (1)

Q Imagine a monster is chasing you.

What would you do?

A I would take a t_________.

(2)

Q Imagine a monster is chasing you.

What would you do?

A I would r_________ away.

7 (1)

Q What would you rather do?

A I would rather do the l_________.

(2)

Q What would you rather do?

A I would rather throw o_________ the trash.

8 (1)

A Tell her what she should do.

B You should wear g_________.

(2)

A Tell him what he should do.

B You should call the b_________ company.

9 (1)

Q What do you think about this class?

A I think m_________ class is fun.

(2)

Q What do you think about this class?

A I think m_________ class is boring.

10 (1)

Q What happened?

A I went to a supermarket last week.
But I didn't have any m________.

(2)

Q What happened?

A Last Friday, I didn't bring my b________ to school.

11 (1)

Q Where did you see this?

A I saw a s________ at the beach.

(2)

Q Where did you see this?

A I saw a f________ e________ on the road.

12 (1) Q What is the last thing you do to draw this?

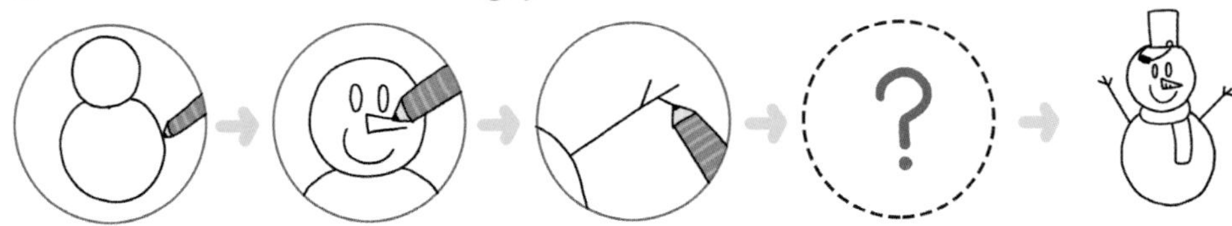

A Last, draw a hat and a s________.

(2) Q What is the last thing you do to make this?

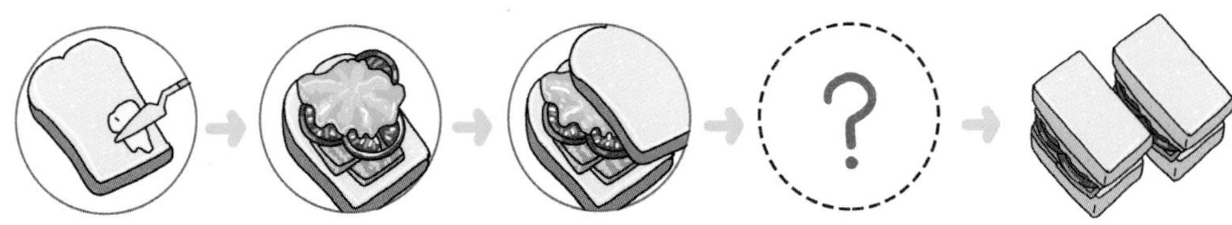

A Last, c________ the sandwich.

13 (1)

Q What is happening?

A A boy is making a s________.

(2)

Q Why is this happening?

A Because it is h________.

14 (1)

Q Do you think Cinderella should punish her stepmother after she marries the prince?

A I d________ because she is a good girl.

(2)

Q Do you think Cinderella should punish her stepmother after she marries the prince?

A I a________ because the stepmother was so mean to her.

Talk to Me 2

2ND Edition

Workbook

◆ Components ◆

Student Book / Workbook

◆ Online Resources ◆

eBook, Audio Files, Lesson Plan, Answer Key, Word List,
Test Sheets, PPTs, and others